THE LIBRARY OF YALE COLLEGE

FROM THE UNIVERSITY QUARTERLY, OCT., 1860.

[NOTE.—In the preparation of a brief sketch of the Library of Yale College, there is little opportunity for originality. Several accounts of this collection of books have already been printed, the best of which, by Mr. Herrick, appeared in Guild's Librarian's Manual; the following article is based upon that. The necessary additions have been made to bring the history down to the present time, and some other amplifications have also been admitted. Prof. Kingsley's Sketch of the History of the College has also been freely used.]

HISTORICAL SKETCH.

ABOVE the main entrance to the Library of Yale College, within the walls of the building, three marble tablets are placed, having inscribed upon them the names of the principal donors to that collection of books. Of these, the central tablet commemorates the foundation of the College as well as the foundation of the Library. Although the story has been often told of the simple ceremonial by which "a collegiate school" was established in Connecticut, i, must be repeated here, for no history of the Library or the College would be complete without it. Ten ministers of the gospel, who had been named by general consent as the trustees of the proposed institution, assembled at Branford in the year 1700, bringing with them a number of books to be presented to the association. The names of these donors (all of whom, except Mr. Buckingham, were graduates of Harvard College,) are as follows:

Rev. James Noyes, of Stonington.
Rev. Israel Chauncy, of Stratford.
Rev. Thomas Buckingham, of Saybrook.
Rev. Abraham Pierson, of Killingworth.
Rev. Samuel Mather, of Windsor.
Rev. Samuel Andrew, of Milford.
Rev. Timothy Woodbridge, of Hartford.
Rev. James Pierpont, of New Haven.
Rev. Noadiah Russell, of Middletown.
Rev. Joseph Webb, of Fairfield.

As each one laid his offering upon the table he said: "I give these books for founding a College in this colony." This has ever been considered, says Prof. Kingsley, the beginning of the College.

About forty volumes were thus collected, the value of which was estimated by President Clap to be thirty pounds sterling. They were committed to the keeping of the minister in whose house they had been brought together, Rev. Samuel Russell, of Branford, a graduate of Harvard College in the class of 1681. He may therefore be regarded as the first Librarian of Yale College.

Among the papers of President Stiles, preserved in the Library, is a volume in which he has recorded, under date of 1784, the names of such of the books given by the original donors as he was able at that time to distinguish. Many, if not all of these volumes, may still be identified. They are chiefly theological works, many of them being of an exegetical character. The remarkable fact has before been noticed, that "among them there was not a single volume relating to classical literature or the sciences." Most of the books were folios, and are bound in plain brown leather.

For the gratification of those who are curious in such matters, we append the list, verbatim, as given by Dr. Stiles:

"BOOKS WITH WHICH THE COLLEGE WAS FOUNDED.

Given by the Reverend Israel Chauncey.

Bezae Tractat. Theol. Fol.
Zonaræ, Annales. Fol.
Funcii Chronologia. Fol.
Catalogus Testium Veritatis. Fol.
Bullingeri Opera. 6 Tomi.

Given by the Reverend Rector Pierson.

Rodolphi Gualteri Homiliae in Prophetas et Johannem et Acta. 4 Vol. Fol.
Thesaurus Scripturae canonicæ.
Pet. Ramus in Artes Liberales.
Tractatus de Literis.
Ecclesiastical Exposition upon the Psalms.
Liber Sermonum.
A Commentary on Matthew.

Pet. Martyri Defensio Eucharistiae.
Flavii Josephi Opera.
Aurelii Augustini Opera.
Augustinus Marloratus in Esaiam.
Erasmus de Ratione concionandi.
Paraphrase on 4 Evang.
An exposition of the N. Test.
Examen concilii Tridentini per Chemnicium.
Liber de Summa Trinitate.

Given by the Reverend James Pierpont.

Biblia Lat. Jun. et Tremel. Fol.
Concordantiae Bibliorum. Fol.
Ferdinandi Quirini de Salazar de beata Virgine. Fol.
Caryl on Job. 4to.
Ravanelli Bibliotheca Sacra. Fol.
Beucer in Psalmos."

The collection of books thus commenced, was kept in Branford three years, and then removed to Killingworth, where the Rector of the College resided. It is supposed that upon his death in 1707, the Library was taken to Saybrook, the seat of the College, where it remained till 1718. The new building erected for the institution in New Haven, was then completed, and the College was established in the latter place. "The removal, however, was not effected without strong opposition," says Prof. Kingsley.* "Forcible resistance was made at Saybrook to the removal of the Library; and the governor and council thought it necessary to assemble at that place, to aid the sheriff in the execution of his duty. Besides other disorders, the carts provided for transporting the books were destroyed at night; the bridges between Saybrook and New Haven were broken down, and in the scramble many valuable books and papers were lost. The Library was about a week on the road."

Early in the century, about one hundred and seventy volumes were sent to the College by Sir John Davie of Groton,

* Prof. Kingsley's Hist. Sketch of Yale Coll., p. 7.

Conn., who was then in England. A large portion of these were his own gift, and the others were contributed by several non-conformist ministers in Devon, and other gentlemen.

In 1714, Jeremiah Dummer, Esq., of Boston, the Colonial agent of Connecticut in England, sent to the College about eight hundred volumes, one hundred and twenty of which were his own donation, and the remainder were such as he had solicited from various contributors, including Governor Yale, Sir Isaac Newton, Sir Richard Steele, Dr. Woodward, Dr. Halley, Dr. Bentley, Dr. Kennet, Dr. Calamy, Dr. Edwards, Rev. Matthew Henry, Mr. Whiston, J. Sheffield, Esq., Sir Richard Blackmore, and many others. The archives of the Library contain a list of this important donation, specifying the books which were given by each benefactor. Sir Isaac Newton presented a copy of his Principia, and also of his Optics, a Greek Lexicon, and the Commentarii of Budaeus; Sir Richard Steele "all the Tatlers and Spectators, being eleven volumes in royal paper, neatly bound and gilt;" Sir Richard Blackmore his poetical works. Pertaining to this last mentioned gift there is extant an interesting letter from Mr. Dummer,* dated Whitehall, May 3, 1713, in which he says: "The Library I am collecting for your College comes on well. Sir Richard Blackmore (to whom I delivered the Committee's letter,) brought me in his own chariot, all his works, in four volumes folio; and Mr. Yale has done something, though very little considering his estate and his relation to the College." Other distinguished writers presented copies of their own works; and through them and the other donors, the resources of the Library in literary and scientific works were very much extended, although in this as in the earlier donations, theological books were more numerous than those of any other department. A little later than this, Governor Yale made another donation of books, not far from three hundred volumes, which were received in 1718; and Mr. Dummer added, at about the same time, seventy-five volumes to his former donation. Twenty three volumes, including several in medicine and surgery, were

---

* Quoted in Dr. Bacon's Hist. Disc., p. 189.

given to the College in 1720 by Dr. Daniel Turner, and ten years later Rev. Dr. Isaac Watts presented copies of his works.

The next important gift which the Library received, was that of the distinguished and liberal Bishop Berkeley, then Dean of Derry in Ireland. During his residence in Newport he had presented to the Library copies of his own works, and now in 1733, he sent to the College from England nearly a thousand volumes, "the finest collection of books which up to that time had ever come at once into America." President Clap, who makes this remark, goes on to say* "I judge that this collection cost at least £400 sterling. This donation of books was made partly out of the doctor's own estate, but principally out of monies which he procured from some generous gentlemen in England. Upon the receipt of them the trustees sent the doctor a letter of thanks, and have since given him repeated expressions of the grateful sense which they retain of his generosity towards this College." There is a manuscript catalogue of this valuable gift preserved in the Library. It includes several copies of the Greek Testament, and of the Delphin editions of Horace, Virgil, Terence, Ovid, Juvenal and Martial, and other classical works, designed, probably, to be used as text books by the students; but the collection is chiefly made up of single copies of standard works in various departments of literature and science, including most of the Greek and Latin Classics, and a set nearly complete of the Christian Fathers. "The Dean had himself selected these books for his contemplated college in Bermuda; they were generally of the most valuable editions, and in the best style of binding. It is worthy of remark, that not a volume of this collection appears to have been put in merely to swell the number; all were evidently sent on account of their intrinsic value."†

The next event of importance in the history of the Library, was the appearance of a printed classified Catalogue, which was prepared in 1743 by President Clap. "Before this time," he remarks,‡ "there never had been any perfect catalogue of the books in the Library; for want of which the students

---

* Clap's Hist. of Yale Coll., p. 138.

† Prof. Kingsley.

‡ Clap's Hist. of Yale Coll., p. 143.

were deprived of much of the benefit and advantage of them. The Rector therefore placed all the books in the Library in a proper order, (but in honor to the Rev. Dr. Berkeley, for his extraordinary donation, his books stood by themselves, at the south end of the Library) and put a number to every book in its proper class and box ; and then took three catalogues of the books, one as they stood in their proper order on the shelves, and another in an alphabetical order, and a third wherein the most valuable books were placed under proper heads, according to the subject matter of them ; together with figures referring to the place and number of each book. By which means it might be easily known what books were in the Library upon any particular subject, and where they might be found with the utmost expedition. This catalogue was printed, and was a great incitement to the diligence and industry of the scholars in reading of them." This catalogue forms a volume of 48 pages, 18mo., and was printed at New London. It is prefaced by a sort of Guide to Reading, prepared by Rev. Samuel Johnson, a graduate of the College in 1714, originally of Stratford, and afterward President of Columbia College in the city of New York. It is entitled "An Introduction to the Study of Philosophy, exhibiting a general view of all the Arts and Sciences, for the use of Students, with a catalogue of some of the most valuable authors necessary to be read in order to instruct them in a thorough knowledge of each of them. By a gentleman educated at Yale College. The Second edition enlarged; the first having been published at London in the Republic of Letters for May, in the year 1731, Art. xxxvii." New London, 1743, 18mo.

During the latter portion of the century the Library did not increase rapidly, either by purchase or donation. President Clap, reviewing the condition of the College in 1765, remarks,* "We have a good Library consisting of about 4000 volumes well furnished with ancient authors, such as the Fathers, Historians and Classicks, many modern valuable books of Divinity, History, Philosophy and Mathematicks, but not many authors who have wrote within these thirty years."

---

* Hist. Yale Coll., p. 86.

Probably there was little improvement in the state of the collection until the country had begun to recover from the effects of the Revolutionary War. Indeed, during the war the Library was sent into the interior to secure it from the enemy, and many valuable books are supposed to have been lost. The most important donations of the period were those of Rev. Dr. Price of London, in 1784, and Rev. Dr. Erskine of Edinburg, each of whom, at different times, between 1788 and 1795, presented several volumes to the College.

A fund for the maintenance of the Library, was commenced in 1763, when a bequest of ten pounds was made by Rev. Jared Eliot, of Killingworth. A like sum was received in 1777 from Rev. Thos. Ruggles of Guilford, and in 1791, a bequest of $1,122, was received from Rev. Samuel Lockwood, D. D., of Andover, Conn. Dr. Lockwood was a graduate of Yale College in 1745. Three years afterward he was settled as a minister in Andover, Conn., where he remained for forty-three years, till his death in 1791. A sketch of his life may be found in the second volume of Dr. Sprague's Annals of the American Pulpit.

In 1807, Hon. Oliver Wolcott, then residing in New York, gave $2,000 to the Library fund. Mr. Wolcott was a graduate of the College in 1788. He succeeded Alexander Hamilton as Secretary of the Treasury of the United States, and was afterwards Governor of Connecticut, an office which both his father and grand-father had previously held.

In 1821, a bequest of $3,000 was made to the College by Noah Linsly, Esq., of Wheeling, Va., but previously of Branford, Conn. By vote of the corporation, the income of this gift was assigned to the Library, and was so continued until the year 1851. Mr. Linsly was a graduate of the College in 1791.

In 1823, a donation of several hundred volumes was made by Rev. Jedediah Morse, D. D., the geographer, and his son Prof. S. F. B. Morse, distinguished as the inventor of the electro-magnetic telegraph, both graduates of the College. The same year, Eli Whitney, Esq., of New Haven, well-known for his invention of the cotton-gin, gave to the fund, $500, the income to be expended in the purchase of books on Practical Mechanics. Daniel Wadsworth, Esq., of Hartford, likewise gave $500, the income to be used for buying books on Natural History and Chemistry.

In 1833, the sum of $5,000 was contributed to the fund, by John T. Norton, Esq., of Albany, N. Y., now of Farmington, Conn.

In 1836, the Library funds were enlarged by a bequest of $10,000, received from Alfred E. Perkins, M. D., of Norwich, Conn. This legacy forms a separate fund, and the income thereof is expended in buying books to be kept apart, and forming a distinct portion of the Library. Several thousand volumes, including many rare and costly works, have already been added to the Library as the result of his bequest. He was born in Norwich, in 1809, and graduated at Yale College in 1830. In 1833, he received the degree of Doctor of Medicine in Philadelphia, and the fairest hopes were entertained of his usefulness and success; but he died in 1834. His munificent gift is the largest which the College Library has ever received, and will remain a perpetual monument of his generosity and public spirit. A portrait in oil, of Dr. Perkins, is among the ornaments of the Library, where it was placed by the liberality of his sister, Mrs. John A. Rockwell, of Norwich.

In 1843, a bequest made in 1825, by Rev. John Elliott, of Guilford, reached the amount of $1,000. By the terms of gift, $50 of the annual income of this fund is to be applied in buying books for the Theological Department.

In 1845, the income of the Library funds having accumulated to a considerable amount, Professor Kingsley, who was the Librarian for nineteen years previous to 1825, and was every way qualified for the undertaking, went abroad and expended in England, Holland, France and Germany, about $8,000 in the purchase of books.

In 1849, a legacy left for the Library fund by Mr. Addin Lewis, of New Haven, (who died in 1842,) reached the intended amount of $5,000, and the annual income has since been applied to the Library.

In 1850, a gift of $500 to the Library fund, resulting from

a previous conditional subscription to another object, was received from Professor Kingsley.

A collection of about four thousand volumes, chiefly in Ecclesiastical History and patristic Theology, formerly belonging to Professor J. K. Thilo, of the University of Halle, who died in 1853, was added to the Library, by purchase, in 1854.

THE LIBRARY BUILDING.

A building for the reception of the Library of the College and the Libraries of the literary societies of the Institution, was commenced in 1842. The College Library was removed in 1843, into one of the smaller apartments, but the principal Hall was not ready for the reception of books until 1846. The building is of Gothic style, and the material is brown sandstone from Portland, Conn. It comprises two Halls for the College Library, with reading-room, ante-room, and Librarian's room connected, and also separate Halls for the Society Libraries. The southern wing is occupied by the Library of the Linonian Society, the northern, by that of the Brothers' Society. The dimensions of the building are as follows; whole front, 151 feet; front of main Hall, 51 feet; length of main Hall, 95 feet; front of each wing, 30 feet; length of each wing, 67 feet; connecting wings, 26 feet by 40 feet; extreme height of towers, 91 feet; interior dimensions of main Hall, 83 feet by 41 feet; height of nave, 51 feet. The entire cost of the structure, when stone pinnacles are added, will be about $40,000.

Previous to the erection of the present Library edifice, the books were kept in a large Hall in the upper story of the Chapel, which has been used by the School of Engineering for several years lately past. Previous to that, an upper room in the Lyceum, afterwards known as the Rhetorical Chamber, (and now divided into recitation rooms,) was appropriated to them; and at a still earlier day the books were kept in the upper story of the old Chapel, now called the Athenæum. Still earlier than this, the first room assigned to the Library, was in the wooden building erected for the College in 1717-18, and pulled down in 1776 and 1782.

LIBRARY FUNDS.

From the review of the History of the College Library which has already been given, it appears that the following funds have been appropriated to its maintenance by the generosity of the persons who are named.

Eliot and Ruggles,	$115 00
Lockwood,	1,122 33
Wolcott,	2,000 00
Whitney,	500 00
Wadsworth,	500 00
Lewis,	5,000 00
Porter,	100 00
Kingsley,	500 00
Elliott,	1,184 29
Norton,	5,000 00
Perkins,	10,000 00
Total,	$26,021.62

The annual income from these sources is about $1,500, which is appropriated to the purchase of books and periodicals; a sum far from adequate to the wants of so large an institution as Yale College.

NUMBER OF VOLUMES IN THE COLLEGE LIBRARY AT DIFFERENT PERIODS.

It is an imperfect way to estimate the value of any Library by the number of volumes which it contains, especially as it is always a matter of doubt how the books should be counted.

The following figures must therefore be considered as only an approximate statement of facts. The Library has contained at different periods, according to the authorities mentioned, the following number of volumes:

In 1700,	40 volumes,	Tradition.
In 1743,	2,600 "	Printed Catalogue.
In 1766,	4,000 "	Clap's Hist. Yale College.
In 1791,	2,700 "	Printed Catalogue.
In 1835,	10,000 "	Kingsley's Sketch of Yale Coll.
In 1845,	10,000 "	

In 1850, 21,000 volumes.
In 1860, 38,000 "

The losses indicated between 1766 and 1791 were occasioned by the removal of the books during the war.

PRESENT NUMBER OF VOLUMES.

The present number of volumes reported as in the College Library, is obtained by actual count of the volumes as they stand upon the shelves, exclusive of unbound pamphlets. A more complete statement of the present number of volumes accessible to the College, would include an enumeration of the three other collections deposited in the building, and of the Medical and Law Libraries, which may be stated as follows :

Library of Yale College, (exclusive of pamphlets,)	38,000	vols.
Linonian Library,	12,000	"
Brothers' Library,	12,000	"
Medical and Law Libraries,	5,000	"
Total,	67,000	

The number of unbound pamphlets is estimated at seven thousand.

The Library of the American Oriental Society, numbering about 1800 separate articles, is kept in the College Library building.

Several of the College Professors have also large and valuable libraries in the specialties to which they are devoted. The collection in Greek literature belonging to President Woolsey, that of Oriental books belonging to Professor Salisbury, the Transactions and Scientific Journals belonging to the Editors of the Journal of Science, Professors Silliman and Dana, and the mathematical Library of Mr. Hillhouse, are deserving of particular mention.

NUMBER OF VOLUMES IN THE SOCIETY LIBRARIES AT DIFFERENT PERIODS.

The Society Libraries, for nearly a hundred years, have been maintained by the voluntary subscriptions and donations of the undergraduated Students.

The Linonian Society, founded in 1753, began its Library in 1769, when the first contribution of books was made by Timothy Dwight, Nathan Hale and James Hillhouse. The last catalogue of this Library was published in 1860. The number of volumes at different periods has been as follows:

In 1770,	100	Volumes.
In 1780,	152	"
In 1790,	330	"
In 1800,	475	"
In 1811,	724	"
In 1822,	1,187	"
In 1831,	3,505	"
In 1837,	5,581	"
In 1841,	7,500	"
In 1846,	10,103	"
In 1860,	12,000	"

The society of the Brothers in Unity, was founded in 1768, and began its Library soon after. The last catalogue of the Library, printed in 1851, states the number of volumes at different periods to have been as follows:

In 1780,	163	Volumes.
In 1808,	723	"
In 1818,	937	"
In 1825,	1,730	"
In 1832,	3,562	"
In 1835,	4,565	"
In 1838,	6,078	"
In 1846,	9,140	"
In 1851,	11,652	"
In 1860,	12,000	"

The Calliopean Society, which was founded in 1819, was disbanded in 1854, and its Library sold, a considerable portion of the books being purchased by the College.

CONDITION OF THE COLLEGE LIBRARY.

Although the College Library is not so large as could be

wished, the selection of books has been made with care for many years past. It is properly a Library of reference; the Libraries of the literary societies being intended for circulation. In purchasing books for the College Library, the effort is made to secure, in the first place, such standard works as are not otherwise accessible in New Haven, and are needed by those connected with the College, who are engaged in researches of a scientific or literary character.

No catalogue has been printed since 1823. There is a manuscript catalogue on cards, but it is not proposed to print it.

The Library has no ancient manuscripts of importance. Among the modern ones which it possesses are about forty volumes left by President Stiles, which are often consulted, being especially valuable in relation to the political and ecclesiastical History of this country. It has also a collection of papers relating to the controversy between the Mohegan Indians and the colony of Connecticut. The papers collected by Dr. Benjamin Trumbull, in the preparation of his History of Connecticut, are also owned by the College.

Among printed books, the following may be mentioned: Graevii Gronovii Thesaurus Antiquitatum, etc. 87 vols. folio; Muratori's Scriptores Italici, 24 vols. folio; Description de l'Egypte, Paris, (an early copy), 1809, etc. 22 vols. folio; Kingsborough's Antiquities of Mexico, 9 vols. folio; Silvestre's Paléographie Universelle, 4 vols. folio; Zahn's Antiquities of Pompeii, Herculaneum and Stabia, folio; Documents Inédits sur l'Histoire de la France, 107 vols. 4to. (in progress); Annali dell' Instituto di Corrispondenza Archeologica, 1829–45, 16 vols. 8vo.; Bulletino do. 1829–44; Maii Scriptorum Veterum Nova Collectio Vaticana, 10 vols. folio; Maii Spicilegium Romanum, 10 vols. 8vo.; Piranesi's Collection of Italian Antiquities, etc. 27 vols. folio; Pertz's Monumenta Germaniæ Historica, vols. 1–12, folio; Fungruben des Orients, 6 vols. folio; Milan edition of the Italian Classics, 400 vols. 8vo.; Allgemeine Literatur Zeitung, complete, 1785–1849, 141 vols. 4to.; Berliner Jahrbücher, complete, 1827–1845, 33 vols. 4to.; Wiener Jahrbücher der Literatur, complete, 1818–1849; Collection of original pamphlets concerning English Affairs from Charles

I. to James II.; Publications of the English Record Commission, 74 vols. folio; Taylor's Translations of Plato and Aristotle, 19 vols. 4to.; Calvin's Opera Omnia, 9 vols. folio; Hansard's Parliamentary Debates, 137 vols. 8vo.; Ternaux-Compans's Collection of Voyages, &c. relative to the Discovery of America, 20 vols. 8vo. Paris; Ersch and Grüber's Encyclopedia, 100 vols. 4to. (in progress); Catesby's Natural History of Carolina, folio; Byzantine Historians, Venice Edition, 23 vols. folio; Dumont D'Urville, Voyage au Pole Sud, 1837–40, 14 vols. royal 8vo., 6 vols. folio; Gould's Humming Birds, folio; Museo Borbonico, 12 vols. 8vo., Gallerie du Palais Pitti, 4 vols. folio; Jones's Grammar of Ornament, folio; Texier's Asia Minor, 3 vols. folio; Purchas, his Pilgrimes, 5 vols. folio, 1625–6.

The Library is well supplied with sets of European Scientific periodicals, including the Transactions of some of the most important Academies and learned societies. Many of those which are still in progress are regularly received and made accessible in the Reading Room.

The oldest printed book in the collection is a copy of two tracts of St. Augustine, (de vita Christiana, etc.) printed by Ulric Zell of Mayence, A. D. 1467. This book, and several other specimens of early typography, are displayed in a glass case in the main room of the Library.

INSCRIPTIONS.

Four Assyrian tablets, with figures in relief and inscriptions in the cuneiform or arrow headed characters, procured in Nineveh by Rev. W. F. Williams, of Mosul, were presented to the Library in 1855, by a few friends of the college. A portion of a column or altar, found in Beirût, bearing an ancient inscription in Greek, was placed in the Library by President Woolsey.

Three Sanskrit inscriptions, probably of the eleventh or twelfth century, the property of the American Oriental Society, are also deposited in the Library. Copies of these inscriptions are published in the sixth volume of the Journal of the Society. A fac-simile copy of the Rosetta Stone was given to the Library in 1859 by Mr. F. P. Brewer.

COINS.

The Library has a collection of about 3000 ancient and modern coins, mostly the gift of various private individuals. They have recently been arranged and catalogued by Mr. Fisk P. Brewer, who has published notices of the collection in the Yale Literary Magazine, Vol. 25, and in the University Quarterly, Vol. 2.

WORKS OF ART.

The main hall of the Library is ornamented with a portrait already mentioned, of Dr. A. E. Perkins, the founder of the Perkins fund, and with busts of President Day, Professor Silliman, Rev. Dr. N. W. Taylor, and I. Town, Esq., by Mr. C. B. Ives of New Haven, Prof. A. M. Fisher, by H. Augur, and Governor W. A. Buckingham, by H. Dexter, Esq. of Boston. There are also copies in marble by Thomas Crawford, of three antique busts, Homer, Demosthenes, and one formerly known as Cicero. They were the gift of Professor Salisbury. A copy in plaster of the newly identified bust of Cicero in the Vatican at Rome, was given to the Library by Mr. B. P. Akers of Rome.

LIBRARIANS.

Previous to the year 1805, the Senior Tutor acted as Librarian. From that time to 1824, the office was filled by Prof. James L. Kingsley. He was succeeded by Prof. J. W. Gibbs, who held the office until 1843. Edward C. Herrick, Esq. was then appointed Librarian, and held the office for fifteen years, till his resignation in 1858. The present incumbent of the post entered upon his duties in 1856.

The Society Libraries have been in charge of undergraduate Librarians until the present year. Each of them is now in charge of a graduate member of the Society, who is also an assistant in the College Library. Mr. Arthur W. Wright is the Linonian Librarian, Mr. Joseph L. Daniels, that of the Brothers' Society.

REGULATIONS.

The hours during which the Library is regularly open, are from 8 A. M., to 1 P. M., daily, except on Sundays and in vacations. During a considerable portion of the year, it is open again in the afternoon.

The persons entitled to *borrow* from the Library are the College Officers, members of the professional and scientific Schools, and of the Junior and Senior Classes in the College; and also such other persons as may receive permission from the Library Committee.

For *consultation,* the Library is open freely to any applicant. Books are sometimes loaned to persons at a distance by permission of the Committee.

The following are Laws of Yale College respecting the Library.

1. The President, Fellows, members of the several Faculties, Graduates resident at the College, members of the Theological, Medical, Law and Philosophical Schools, and Seniors and Juniors, shall have the liberty of drawing books from the Library. Other persons may have the privilege of consulting the Library, and of drawing books therefrom, by obtaining the permission of the Library Committee. No person shall borrow any book from the Library without the knowledge or presence of the Librarian, and no persons except the President and Librarian shall have a key to the Library. Before being permitted to take away any book, all persons except the President, Fellows and members of the Faculties, shall be required to subscribe an engagement to conform to all the Laws and Regulations of the Library, and to make good all damage or loss thereto which they may occasion or permit.

2. The Library shall be open for the delivery of books during five hours of each secular day of the week in term time, except the week next previous to Commencement, days of public fast and thanksgiving, fourth of July, and such other public days as may be determined upon by the Library Committee. The said Committee shall regulate the opening of the Library during vacations, and shall appoint the hours of opening in term time. The members of the Senior and Junior classes shall have the liberty of drawing and consulting the books of the Library only on Mondays and Thursdays. Those persons who have special permission to draw books from the Library, shall also be allowed to consult books in the Library Rooms, under such regulations as the Committee shall prescribe.

3. The Librarian shall register all books which may be borrowed from the Library, noting the name of the borrower, the title and size of the book, the time when borrowed and when returned. No person shall without permission lend to another a book which he has borrowed

from the Library, nor let it go from his possession; and no person shall, without permission of the Library Committee, carry a book be longing to the Library, out of the town of New Haven, on penalty of being deprived of the use of the Library for a time not exceeding six months, or of paying a fine not exceeding one dollar, at the discretion of said Committee.

No person, except members of the Faculties, may keep more than three volumes from the Library at one time, without permission from the Library Committee.

4. Certain books, which on account of their character or their value, ought not to be removed from the Library, shall be so designated by the Library Committee, and shall not be taken out without their special permission.

5. The members of the Senior and Junior classes and members of the Medical, Law and Scientific schools shall pay for the use of books borrowed from the Library twelve cents for the term of two weeks, or less time for each folio or quarto volume, and six cents for an octavo or smaller volume.

Previous to borrowing books from the Library, members of these schools shall each deposit with the Librarian the sum of five dollars, or a bond from one of the Professors of the College or other responsible person, for the safe keeping and return of the books they may borrow: the money or bond to be surrendered whenever the account is satisfactorily settled. But those who are permitted to draw books from the Library may consult them free of charge in the Library apartments. The Librarian shall have power to remit, in certain cases, at his discretion, charges for the use of books borrowed.

All books borrowed from the Library, except by members of the Faculties and of the Corporation, shall be returned or renewed within two weeks from the time when they are taken; and such books shall also be returned on the Monday next before the end of the first and second terms. Those who fail to return or to renew, at the required time, the books they have borrowed, shall forfeit the use of the Library until such books are returned. The Librarian or his assistant is authorized to limit at his discretion in the case of certain books, the time during which they may be kept from the Library. The sums due for books thus borrowed shall be annually inserted in the July term bills.

Whoever shall borrow a book from the Library shall pay at the discretion of the President or Librarian, for all injury done to it while in his possession. In case of the loss of a volume, the borrower shall be required to replace the same, or pay the value thereof in money;

or if the volume be one of a set, he shall replace the set or pay the value thereof.

All books borrowed from the Library shall be returned thereto one week before Commencement, and whosoever shall, without special permission from the Library Committee, retain books contrary to this law, shall forfeit his right to the use of the Library, during such retention.

6. It shall be the duty of the Librarian to arrange the books in the Library; to cause them to be repaired when necessary; to keep a catalogue of all books presented, or purchased with monies appropriated by the donors for the use of the Library.

At each Commencement, the Librarian shall return to the Corporation a list of the books which have been purchased during the preceding year; and shall report the names of such members of the Senior class as have books from the Library, that their Degrees may be withheld.

7. All books for the Library shall be purchased under the direction of the Library Committee, and shall be deposited in the Library.

8. The Library Committee shall have power to make any regulations for the management of the Library, which they may find necessary, and which shall not be inconsistent with the foregoing Laws.

II. It shall be the duty of the Faculty to exercise supervision over all the Society Libraries admitted into the Library building, to acquaint themselves by inspection or otherwise with the character of the books, to ascertain and if necessary limit the expenditure for Library purposes, and in general, provide for the care and safety of the rooms and libraries deposited therein. It shall be the duty of the several societies, to whom rooms may be assigned in the Library building, through their Librarians or other officers, to afford all facilities for the inspection of their rooms and libraries as the Corporation or Faculty may direct, and to furnish from time to time all such information as the Faculty may require concerning the condition and management of the Libraries. The rooms so assigned to the several societies may be occupied by them until needed for the College Library, or so long as the President and Fellows shall see fit. Such rooms shall be used for Library purposes and for no other. No meetings of the Societies shall be held in them, nor shall they be used as reading rooms except under the direction of the College Inspector or Prudential Committee. And if these regulations or any of them are violated, the Faculty may, if they see fit, punish the person or persons in fault, or may require the Society in whose room such violations occur, to remove the books to some other place.

www.ingramcontent.com/pod-product-compliance
Lightning Source LLC
LaVergne TN
LVHW020638110826
845149LV00004B/1259
9781418191344